Excluding the Jew Within Us

Excluding the Jew Within Us

Jean-Luc Nancy

Translated by Sarah Clift

polity

Originally published in French as *Exclu le juif en nous* by Jean-Luc Nancy. Copyright © ÉDITIONS GALILEE 2018

This English edition © Polity Press, 2020

Polity Press
65 Bridge Street
Cambridge CB2 1UR, UK

Polity Press
101 Station Landing
Suite 300
Medford, MA 02155, USA

ISBN-13: 978-1-5095-4272-7 (hardback)
ISBN-13: 978-1-5095-4273-4 (paperback)

A catalogue record for this book is available from the British Library.

Library of Congress Cataloging-in-Publication Data
Names: Nancy, Jean-Luc, author. | Clift, Sarah, translator.
Title: Excluding the Jew within us / Jean-Luc Nancy ; translated by Sarah Clift.
Other titles: Exclu le juif en nous. English
Description: English edition. | Cambridge, UK ; Medford, MA : Polity, 2020. | "Originally published in French as Exclu le juif en nous by Jean-Luc Nancy. Copyright © Éditions Galilée 2018." | Includes bibliographical references and index. | Summary: "A leading philosopher argues that anti-Semitism is rooted in the structures of Western thought"-- Provided by publisher.
Identifiers: LCCN 2020001435 (print) | LCCN 2020001436 (ebook) | ISBN 9781509542727 (hardback) | ISBN 9781509542734 (paperback) | ISBN 9781509542741 (epub) Subjects: LCSH: Antisemitism--Philosophy. Classification: LCC DS145 .N2713 2020 (print) | LCC DS145 (ebook) | DDC 305.892/4001--dc23
LC record available at https://lccn.loc.gov/2020001435
LC ebook record available at https://lccn.loc.gov/2020001436

Typeset in 12.5 on 15 pt Adobe Garamond by
Servis Filmsetting Ltd, Stockport, Cheshire
Printed and bound in Great Britain by CPI Group (UK) Ltd, Croydon

For further information on Polity, visit our website: politybooks.com

Contents

CONTENTS

Preface to the English Edition

I put the finishing touches on this text for the English translation of this book in early November 2018, just days after the most serious antisemitic attack in US history took place, on October 27 in Pittsburgh. Evidently, imitators are *still* emboldened by the anathemas of John Chrysostom, the diatribes of Luther, the rantings in *Protokoly Mędrców Syjonu* [*The Protocols of the Elders of Zion*], and the ideology of *Mein Kampf* to claim that "the Jews are children of Satan" before shooting them in the middle of an American city whose motto is *benigno numine* ("by a benevolent divine power," "by the favor of heaven").

This rapid geographical expansion of

antisemitic violence might be seen as the symptom of a general increase in incidents of impulsive or impassioned violence (insofar as this type can be distinguished from others, for example social, economic, or political violence) that are taking place in a disoriented world. But, even if that were the case, it still has to be understood in terms of its stupefying continuity with, and continuation of, a disease and a derangement that has belonged to the West since its very inception.

That this is how such a ferocious hatred, unique in the history of civilizations, would reach the continent and country where the West underwent its most major expansion before spreading everywhere—this is what gives the present book its horrible justification: to expose the originary and constitutive role played by antisemitism in the development of the symbolic, ethical, and emotional structure of this West.

Introduction

The work undertaken here consists of uncovering at least one of the sources—no doubt the main one—of the phenomenon of antisemitism, as it has continued and intensified over the last twenty-two centuries and as it stubbornly continues to resurface well into the twenty-first century—in Europe, but also in North America, where it is not new but is being reactivated, and in South America, where it seems to be reignited by issues related to Israel and Palestine.

The present study locates the deep origin of antisemitism—this entirely unique phenomenon in the history of civilizations—within a division created in the European world. An originary division, as it were, which also means a divided origin or a division at the origin. The two meanings must be explored and examined together; and the present essay is meant to be a preliminary foray into this work.

Nonetheless, it will be clear to everyone that the hideous gash that the extermination of the Jews has inflicted on the history of Europe shall always remain tethered to that history: when it has resurfaced elsewhere, it has done so in derivative and never comparable forms. In producing the West, Europe has certainly spread a great many of its features throughout the world, but its delirious and mythic racial fury could never export what tied that fury to the intense desire to regenerate and rebuild Europe.[1] In a sense, the discovery of what would come to be called "the New World" initiated a new generative process and, in that sense, diverted the original anxiety.

This is why I cannot forego a new introduction to the first version of this book in English. Not only must the question be situated within a context other than that of Europe, but this change in perspective will allow me to verify the analysis of Europe itself.

There are many features that make the invasion and conquest of the American continent beginning in the fifteenth century not only an expansion of Europe but also a break from it, or from the continuity of European history—a break whose decisive mark is the independence of the United States, followed by the multiple independences of Latin America. Among such features, I must emphasize the foundational character of these independences. The gesture of breaking from the European states is itself inseparable from the gesture of founding: it is the beginning of another history. Whatever dissimilarities there are between the independence of the Thirteen Colonies and those that followed, these acts will all have been of a different nature from the acts of founding the European states: from Russia to England or Sweden, despite important differences, they all emerged from under the shadow of the Roman Empire. This was Europe's true starting point: Rome was its own foundation, or at least this is how it understood itself. One could say that Greece invented autonomy—breaking with the old autochthonies—and that Rome invented a new autochthony: that of an empire founded above particular peoples, in a power that is both autocratic and virtually universal.

This is how Rome gets divided into two, the

celestial and the earthly—the first tending to get conflated with a heavenly Jerusalem, in view of which it becomes necessary to wipe out the earthly Jerusalem, that is, the other way of practicing autonomy: according to a covenant with an absolute other and according to a call rather than a founding.

With America, the shadow of Rome receded. North America believed itself to be founded by divine right—"divine" being understood here as its human right to establish its own autonomy. In the 1776 Declaration of Independence, the task was for the Thirteen States "to assume among the powers of the earth, the separate and equal station to which the Laws of Nature and of Nature's God entitle them." In a certain way, there was greater kinship here with the Jewish representation than with the Christian. Moreover, in the backdrop to 1776, the Puritan culture of the founding fathers aligned them in striking ways with Jews in exile from the Promised Land.

For its part, most of Latin America followed the logic of European sovereignty, that is, the logic of a parallelism of two powers, the civil and the religious, as closely related to each other as they are fundamentally distinct. In Europe this logic always divided the idea of the Jews into a civil affiliation, which imagined a religious shift taking place over time, and a religious exclusion, which had weighty civil repercussions. When Spain expelled its Jews, those who reached America (often as Marranos) were allowed to stay because the vice-royalty was not operating in the same context as royalty was: Catholicism had been exposed to so many different cultures, beliefs, and conditions there that Judaism could more easily be forgotten.

*

So, for very different reasons, the two configurations of the New World did not import the antisemitism that was infecting Europe throughout that period. Of course, antisemitism was still present and ready to be reactivated, as it most emphatically was during the communist revolution, which was largely framed as the Jews' doing. Long before that, in 1790, antisemitism was already enough of a problem that George Washington, the first president of the United States, felt it necessary to pit the civil religion of the United States against the legacy of hatred of the Jews, in the following admonition:

The Government of the United States, which gives to bigotry no sanction, to persecution no assistance, requires only that they who live under its protection should demean themselves as good citizens in giving it on all occasions their effectual support. [. . .]

May the children of the stock of Abraham who dwell in this land continue to merit and enjoy the good will of the other inhabitants—while every one shall sit in safety under his own vine and fig tree and there shall be none to make him afraid.

May the father of all mercies scatter light, and not darkness, upon our paths, and make us all in our several vocations useful here, and in His own due time and way everlastingly happy.

This text comes from a letter that Washington addressed to the Jewish community of Newport.[2] Some people of note in this community traded slaves. So goes the story. In the twenty-first century, Claudio Magris can write: "Are Jews the blacks of the world and the blacks in America the Jews in Egypt, persecuted by the Pharaoh because he fears them?"[3] This sentence, written no later than 2015, echoes the new epidemic of antisemitism that continues to gain ground around the world, in America as well as in Europe, in Russia (despite official efforts), and in the Muslim world—not to mention the Chinese and Japanese versions of Jewish conspiracy theories, all stemming from the *Protocols of the Elders of Zion*.

It is noteworthy how often and how forcefully the antisemitism that is currently spreading throughout the globalized world is accused of being anti-American—just as antisemitism in America used to be accused of being anticommunist. In both cases, the accusation involves world domination: the Jew is the soul or essence of a will—often literally referred to as diabolical—to subject the planet to the law of its greedy calculations. It does not matter what hue or tone this will to dominate adopts here or there: the Jew takes on all manner of roles or disguises, since she has nothing of her own beyond her voracious rapacity.

*

As we know, in America (in the United States, Argentina, Brazil, etc.), Judaism has been able more than anywhere else to develop a culture that is both distinctly its own *and* integrated into its environment (the latter being more often the case in the rest of the world). Frequently this culture is also an interested party in questions concerning American power, even to the point of contesting it or generating disputes about it. Nor did it remain silent about what America calls "the Holocaust," which Europe replaced with "Shoah." However, in spite of what could be said about the role played by the two Americas in this event, the fact remains that it was the Jews of Europe who were exterminated and that Europe is the place from which we can attempt to discern the extent of this antisemitic gash, constitutive of Europe, by going back to the very beginning.

Thus, paying attention to the Americas, where so many Jews expelled from Europe found refuge from the fifteenth to the twentieth centuries, contributes to a better understanding of the nature and stakes of what, it seems to me, when we speak of hatred for the Jews we must describe as constitutive—decisive, structural, essential, historial—of Europe and of what would have energized the civilization we still call western, even though we now tend to understand it as universal.

I

Banality

Antisemitism is constantly recurring. The extermination of Jews in Europe was enough to make
one think that, seventy-five years later, "the
belly from which it came out"—as Brecht once
wrote—could not possibly still be fertile. But it
is.

It is not recurring in the form of camps, or
a "night of broken glass" [*Kristallnacht*], or
anti-Jewish laws. Laws are even being passed in
Europe that prohibit antisemitic language and
acts. Nonetheless, what returns is doing so in a
manner that made it possible, not so very long
ago, for some twenty European countries to subject Jews to state persecution—namely in the
mode of banality.

In recent years newspapers have taken to using sobriquets such as "commonplace," "casual," or "everyday" more and more frequently, as a way of decrying the recurrent antisemitism we are witnessing. The use of these terms is not meant to diminish it but rather to deplore its expansion, the (relative) tolerance that surrounds it, and especially its insidious penetration into the consciousness or the unconscious of many of our contemporaries. This fact of language is surprising, given how sharply it contrasts with the criticism Hannah Arendt received, not too long ago, for her use of the phrase "banality of evil," which she most probably developed from Joseph Conrad's preface to his novel *Under Western Eyes*.

At that time it was said that the phrase trivialized the exceptional horror of the genocide. It may be true that Arendt was misled by Eichmann's defence, which rested on claims that he was just a simple bureaucrat carrying out orders. But she was certainly not mistaken about how utterly banal the vulgarity of antisemitism had become in Europe in those days. And, come to think of it, Eichmann's defense was itself based on this terrible banality.

Even today, as is clear from the case of

Heidegger, to speak of "banality" is to be immediately suspected of downplaying or, worse still,
of celebrating antisemitism. However, the banality in question in no way makes it excusable; on
the contrary, its existence attests to a process of
banalization, that is, to a passive acceptance of
stereotypes that emerge from the unfathomable
depths of hatred.

The case of Heidegger is exemplary. The person
capable of developing an idea of the "people" that
is diametrically opposed to any biologism of race
(and, in that sense, also opposed to Nazism) is the
same person who, all the while, would resort to
contemptible racial prejudices about Jews, such as
their would-be gift for scheming, or their finan-
cial greed. It is certainly difficult to see how such
characteristics, if they are going to be considered
real, would not indeed be biological or instinctive.
Otherwise they would have had to be manufac-
tured for the purposes of condemnation—and
this is precisely what they are.

In making such a move, Heidegger buoyed up
an elevated and esoteric thinking by collecting
what was drifting along on the streams of the
most commonplace, widespread, vulgar, or ordinary antisemitism that infected public attitudes

of the time . . . and that continues to infect our own.

Not only does antisemitism continue to infect public attitudes; it has even increased, or been intensified, through the introduction of a Muslim antisemitism, itself arising out of problems that surround the State of Israel—a state whose own founding was no stranger to antisemitism and to the European nationalisms of the nineteenth and twentieth centuries. Unlike Christian countries, Islamic countries had not known virulent antisemitism until the end of the nineteenth century, when European premises and attitudes began to penetrate the "progressive" circles of the Ottoman Empire.

Today an antisemitism circulates all around the Mediterranean—and, more widely, throughout the world—that has become banal again; that is, it feeds on beliefs and images produced over the course of a very long history, in which modern forms have mostly taken over from ancient ones. The latter—often labeled "anti-Judaism"—emerged first and foremost out of religious condemnations and their consequences (exclusion from many sectors, social statutes, professions). Modern forms—bio-ethnological racism and global conspiracy theories—come together in what Hannah Arendt characterizes as the making of an abstract figure, "the Jew," bearer of all flaws and perpetrator of all evils.

Among the many characteristics that clearly indicate continuity between the ancient and the modern, banality must be emphasized: at each stage, what is at stake is the banalization of motifs and motives of ecclesiastical, political, theological, or anthropological origin. It is truly remarkable that intellectual developments throughout history have been able to spread in such a way as to form a self-evident cluster of popular images, in the most banal and low-brow culture as well as in the most elevated (for example in Dante, Shakespeare, Kant, Kierkegaard, Marx, Baudelaire, Heidegger).

Banalization presupposes an assimilation, an intimate incorporation, in the same way in which it has become banal, for instance, to operate a device as sophisticated as the telephone. It therefore presupposes a capacity for absorption that is itself fed by a powerful energy. Hatred for the Jews at first, then invention of a universal Jew who is at once conspiratorial and parasitic: both draw on a powerful resource. Its concealment in our culture is necessary for the latter to be able to produce such a far-reaching, incessant, and virtually intransigent phenomenon.

When we criticize the expression "banality of evil" for minimizing the evil, it is in order to assert the exceptionally monstrous nature of this evil. And this monstrosity is indisputable. At the same time, though, without seeking to relativize in any way the horror of the extermination of the Jews[4] or ceasing to denounce it, we must ask ourselves whether a kind of inverted banality is not also taking place now, consciously or not: precisely the inverted banality of a denunciation that would serve as the last word, and so would be off limits for further research and exploration.

Indeed, the constant repetition of this kind of inverted banality, which consists of denouncing fascisms (most often along with other regimes designated as "totalitarian") as absolute evils, *also* seems to guarantee a self-righteousness that does not need to search any further. "To search further" means here to focus on the conditions of possibility offered within democracies and within culture or civilization for this sudden occurrence. It means asking oneself whether this occurrence simply fell from heaven (or rather arose from hell), or whether it did not find certain resources in the fissures of democracy, humanism, technologism, and economism.

In this respect as well, the case of Heidegger is exemplary. We are very quick to point out that he was a Nazi, and therefore his entire oeuvre must be as well; but we read little or nothing of the work he wrote explicitly or implicitly against Nazism. To be sure, he wrote that work in the name of what Lacoue-Labarthe has called "archi-fascism." But this archi-fascism was itself made possible at that time by the collapse of philosophy into the soft thinking of "values." (Besides, most of the professional philosophers in Germany sided with the prevailing ideology, voluntarily or not, in a very banal way).

It is completely banal to repeat this anti-fascist refrain. But, to stick to the subject of this essay, one should at least ask oneself how it is that antisemitic banality persists so stubbornly in the middle of a world supposedly delivered from fascism. Which leads me back to the question, or the inkling, of how abhorrence for the Jews is implicated in the very genesis of the West.

2

Historial and spiritual

In 1986, in *Heidegger, Art, and Politics: The Fiction of the Political*, Philippe Lacoue-Labarthe described antisemitism as historial and spiritual. He put each of these terms in quotation marks.[5] The context was that of an analysis of politics in Heidegger. This book was noticed, but I do not know whether its description of antisemitism specifically was taken up or engaged with. Of course, Philippe knew nothing about the *Black Notebooks*.

Some thirty years later, the expression "historial antisemitism" would suggest itself to the publisher of these notebooks, Peter Trawny, as fit for capturing what Heidegger claims to be the metaphysical nature of the relation of the Jews to the West. A flurry of criticism was unleashed against Trawny, accusing him of trying to elevate an antisemitism that was in reality as banal, vulgar, coarse, and violent as that found in the *Protocols of the Elders of Zion* (an assessment that did not stop Trawny's critics from mentioning it). No one referred to Lacoue-Labarthe's text.

This is a striking example of how inconsistent public opinions can be, even those supposedly coming from the most knowledgeable commentators or observers. Sometimes we do not know how to read because we are all too prone to rehashing presumed certainties. So at certain times we have only one eye open and at other times we look at things through the wrong lens.

Neither Lacoue-Labarthe nor Trawny ever presumed that Heidegger could be immune to the harshest judgment, that of antisemitism. Both, however, in very different ways and in very different contexts, felt that the philosophical inscription of antisemitism should be taken into account—and it was an account for which, it must be emphasized, Lacoue-Labarthe did not need any other texts beyond what was available at the time.

What do the labels that Lacoue-Labarthe used

in 1986 suggest? The first, "historial," suggests that antisemitism is part of a deep structure of the historical–metaphysical constitution of the West. The second, which is particularly striking in someone who hated any kind of spiritualism, suggests that what is at stake falls under the essential tendencies of a culture or civilization.

The first label takes Pascal at his word: "their history in its duration comprehends all our histories" [*Pensées*, 9.612]—and in fact turns this duration into the enigma of this history itself.

The second label demands that we look at the enigma differently from Pascal or, for that matter, differently from anyone else up until today.

What is involved here is nothing other than the fact that antisemitism is not simply on the order of racism, religion, or social, economic, political, and cultural issues. In other words it cannot simply be grasped in the empirical register but requires a fundamental one[6]—"historial," then, and "spiritual," if we are in truth to place ourselves under the sign of Lacoue-Labarthe's very powerful intuition.[7]

Let us just add that the quotation marks were meant to indicate the insufficient and even problematic character of the terms used and the difficulty of finding substitutes for them. No doubt we should still discuss these terms today; but this is not my intention here. I understand them in the simplest and most direct way. Antisemitism must be called "historial" and "spiritual" because the hate that animates it is rooted in the spiritual and historical (one might say, awkwardly, civilizational) configuration where the West took shape. We cannot account for the one without untangling the other, insofar as it is possible to untangle what brings about great transformations in world history. Whether this history is a destiny or not and whether "spirit" (as opposed to "matter") is a dubious idea are questions for later.

On the other hand, it should be noted that the intuition whose stakes I am trying to grasp here contrasts sharply—unless I am mistaken—with all the best analyses devoted to antisemitism. I am content to recall those of Adorno and Horkheimer, Poliakov, Arendt, and Milner: for all their power and finesse, these analyses have not really opened up the question of the "historial–spiritual." By no means is this meant to be a criticism: western consciousness itself required a long period of maturation or fermentation before concerning itself with a source of antisemitism that is older and deeper than anything we were able to explore in anti-Judaism, in the history of "assimilation," with its multiple stages and aspects, in the area of conspiracy theories, and, finally, in murderous racist frenzies. All these approaches are necessary, but they all indicate a more remote origin—more in the logical than in the historical sense.

To confirm the spiritual and historial character of antisemitism, it would be necessary to spend more time than I have here on the importance of Russian antisemitism. Very old and very much present in orthodox writings, but intensified by the movements of nineteenth-century society, this antisemitism drove many Jews fleeing pogroms to Western Europe (and to the United States). As a result, European antisemitism worsened. Within the constitution of Orthodox Christianity—oriented as it was more toward the Spirit Pantocrator than the incarnated Son, even as it had close links with the idea of a people and a proper "soul"—it is possible to discern a certain tendency to reject a Judaism that was considered all the more loathsome the closer it was.

3

Autoimmunity

All societies, cultures, or civilizations have experienced enmity or hostility toward outside groups. The very idea of the proper (native, familiar) as opposed to the foreigner (without common ties, not of the house—*metoikos* in ancient Greek) is inseparable from sociality. All societies or peoples have also known, and still know, the phenomenon of a more or less pronounced discrimination of certain groups for the benefit of one or two classes, castes, or dominant categories. In other words, each people—in the sense of the identity of a social body that understands itself as such—experiences an impulse toward distinction or exclusion from others or other peoples (themselves understood in the same way).

The necessity of this impulse is not very mysterious, even if a civilization that seems today to have its rightful place anywhere in the world affirms the opposite need, for a mutual recognition of differences. This kind of recognition, however, is supposed to restrain hostility or to get the better of it; it does not deny the possibility of its occurrence. Is it not essential for a group to assert itself, even though its internal multiplicity makes this affirmation an aspiration more than a given (or maybe a given of which this aspiration forms a part?). To be capable of including, one must of necessity exclude.

Individual identifications are not exempt from similar complexities. Individuals, however, have their separation given to them or imposed upon them. For the people, it is a matter of recognizing itself through the diversity of its components. True, individual identity is not entirely given either. It aspires to be itself as well. But it also aspires to be itself, in part, as a desire to belong to a group—which is precisely not the case with the group. Otherwise the very idea of a group would lose its meaning.

My intention here is not to analyse further the highly complex reality of the group or its modes of distinguishing itself or of making an identity for itself. It is to consider a singular case, which stands out among the set of complexities and difficulties in the relations between groups. One civilization alone—the one that used to be European before becoming global, largely as a result of its practical characteristics—actually knew, almost from the beginning, an internal exclusion that has continuously renewed itself for twenty-two centuries: the ignomy of the Jewish people, the modern form of which is called "antisemitism."

Antisemitism stands out in three respects: first, for what has remained unchanged about it up until now; second, in that it has led to the extermination of European Jews by a regime (assisted by others) that made the absolute superiority of an alleged "Aryan race" the metaphysical—and thus also the political—truth of the world; and, finally, because it designates the Jew not as a stranger so much as a pernicious agent within the group and the civilization to which that agent—the Jew—belongs. In the best case, the Jew is seen as an aberration; in the worst case, as a threat enclosed within the whole of which he is a part.

The Jew (I will use this designation for now,

even if it means having to question its constitution) is neither another group nor a member of the in-group. He or she is still part of the group, but in the same way as a pathogenic organ can still be part of a body it infects, or at least threatens to infect. The Jew thus occupies the position of an autoimmune agent: it turns against the immunity of the body to which it belongs. Just as all vertebrates now have latent autoimmunity, so too does the European—now "western"— organism have a self-threatening constitution. This perilous necessity ends up conferring a fateful character on the Jewish people: regardless of a reason, this people is destined to its own misfortune (Ahasver, "the wandering Jew"), just as it is destined to cause the misfortune of others (Süss).[8]

4

Extermination

The current state of the biological sciences allows immunity to be used as a metaphor, but there is of course nothing biological about the metaphor—no more than there is anything actually scientific about the considerations of race and evolution that turned anti-Judaism into anti-semitism during the nationalist, imperialist, and scientist nineteenth century. Deep down, almost nothing has changed. It bears repeating: what belongs to the very origins of our civilization has simply been dressed up in modern rags.

To be sure, modern antisemitism has unleashed some particularly hideous and terrifying energies. We have yet to understand what this particularity is all about. Many discussions have taken place regarding the specific (or non-specific), the incomparable or indeed absolutely unique (or not) nature of this extermination—now designated, at least in Europe, by the Hebrew term "Shoah" (as a common noun, *shoah* means "ruin," "annihilation"), while the word "Holocaust" prevails among English speakers, its Greek etymons designating a complete (*hol-*) burning (*kaein > kaustos*), usually of a large number of animal victims in a sacrifice. In both cases, a common noun became a proper name, capitalized.

When we stick to a common noun such as "extermination," in order to prevent any kind of sanctification or sacralization, it is nonetheless necessary to prefix it by some reference to "Jewishness" (the Jews, the Jewish people), itself then further detailed by specifying that this people comes from Europe. It is also important to remember that this people was not the only one in this situation and that the fate of Roma people is similar in more than one respect (ethnic or middle-eastern character, ancient history, independence from nations, social exclusion). The Roma, on the other hand, do not represent a continuity of religious belonging in the way the Jews do, nor are they implicated in the nascent West in a comparable way, even if they do bear witness to a European dissonance of a similar kind. One could extend this last remark to the Slavs—another ethnic group targeted by the Nazis as an inferior race—as well as to groups in the Nazi camps that were victimized for non-"ethnic" reasons. In what way can homosexuals, communists, and Jehovah's witnesses be said to present analogies with the Jews? In some respects, the analogy here involves nothing more than these groups' divergence or distance from the established order. In the case of communists or other socialists, it turns out that sometimes the individuals concerned are also Jews (they then wear double insignia in the camp). In all cases, they are despised for their inferiority, for their perversity, and even for their morbidity. But it is as if the model or mold of stigmatization were first provided by the treacherous and deicidal Jew before it acquired other distinguishing features.

It is also important to remember that the double genocide of the Jewish and Roma peoples was preceded by events that are difficult not to see as antecedents: first, the genocidal and concentrationary practices of the British on the one hand, of the Germans in South Africa on the other;

and, second, the Armenian genocide. Despite substantial differences, what can be considered a forerunner in all these cases has to do with the systematic organization of practices geared toward exterminating entire peoples or populations. And there is clear evidence to suggest that there are predecessors even to these precursors themselves, since inter-group hostility is practically immemorial. But the twentieth century lent this hostility a veneer of rationality that was both theoretical (racism) and practical (logistics). It also endowed it with features or excuses of industrial productivity through which group hostility could be transformed into world domination—transformed, that is, precisely by the civilization of industry and logistics.

This trend toward domination tends to suppress everything that cannot be transformed as it suits. Everything that impedes the progress of the program of domination—slowness, heaviness, disease, death, ignorance, weakness, malignancy, nuisance—must be overcome or transformed. The defining feature of antisemitism in comparison to all forms of racism is that it finds or traces in "the Jew" a figure that incorporates all these obstacles to the growth of mastery. In this sense, antisemitic hostility is quite far removed from racist hostility: it has less to do with a relationship between groups than with the self-relation of a power that wants to be superior to all groups. Universal to the point of cosmopolitanism, Europe suppresses those who maintain their particularity; however—or, indeed, as a consequence—the stateless Jew is also the enemy of a beautiful and healthy cooperation between nations.

5

Omnipotence

These considerations lead back to what, specifically, distinguishes the extermination of the Jews. It takes place on the inside of and from within Europe and, while that is also the case with the Armenian genocide, the latter does not harken back to the entirety of Europe's past, including the period of classical antiquity. For its part, the stigmatization and persecution of Jews can be found all along the events and the entire expanse of what was invented, propagated, and imposed from the Roman center.

As we know, this center fused together three elements: Greek logos, Latin technique, and Jewish monotheism. The resulting alloy was named Christianity and imperialism, that is, a double structure, ordered to infinity: the infinite in actuality [*l'infini en acte*] of a divine omnipotence and the infinite in becoming [*l'infini en devenir*] of a complete mastery of the world.

We never pay enough attention to the delicate alchemy of this alloy. Infinite power is what binds it: in heaven and on earth, it is only ever about that power. Logos, technique, and the revealed god constitute its three major aspects. All other cultures clearly separate the powers of the gods from the obligations of humans. Our culture organizes an entire universe of power in which divine energy is communicated to humans, who reproduce it by re-creating the world.

Globality is the decisive phenomenon here: with Rome, law, urban planning, and the military camp, a world emerges that encompasses local realities and their forms of belonging. After Rome, a "people" will never again have the all-encompassing meaning of autochthony. The Roman people measures itself in accordance with a common amplitude that tends toward the unlimited.

This common measure includes the feature of self-sufficiency from the Greek logos: the pledge, or the will, to account (or reason)—and to account for everything, beginning with one-self (calculation, speech, the law, power). Greek reason, however, refers beyond itself ("beyond what is," as Plato says). Its autonomy will not work without the heteronomy of this "beyond." In Greek thought, it takes the form of a disqualification of the gods and their myths, opening up the possibility of one sole divine entity that transcends all forms of divinity (Plato is not the only one to evoke it).

Rome ignores this transcendence. As soon as it starts being overtaken by its own power, it also becomes the site of a spiritual worry and agitation. The worries of philosophers, the agitation of the Magi, and initiations into mysteries—all testify to this anxiety at every possible opportunity. The omnipotence that has been set in motion senses that it demands more of itself than it can provide.

At the same time, something is happening outside Greece and Rome—not far away, mind you, and early enough to spread throughout the Mediterranean region. This is the Jewish event. Like the Greek event, it, too, comes about through the collapse of the entire world that precedes it, of palace empires and systems. But it embodies a kind of reverse side of self-sufficiency: it invents an unprecedented mode of belonging.

One might venture to say that the Greco-Roman world both had to and wanted to belong only to itself. It petered out, though, and got lost in itself. It needed another mode of belonging, but one that, despite everything, would restore its self-sufficiency. This is what happened with Christianity. A disconcerted subject regained its self-confidence by trusting an unshakable omnipotence. *Interior intimo meo* ["more inward than my innermost"] and *superior summo meo* ["higher than my uppermost," Augustine].

6

Revelation

In the Iron Age (the age, too, of cities and alphabetic writing), the gods withdrew from the Greek world—which was fully aware of this withdrawal and devoted all its resources to facing up to it. Politics, figurative art, tragedy, and philosophy are products of and witnesses to this expenditure of energy. Each of these spheres, and even the distinctions between them, constitute one aspect of the mutation whereby a replacement or a substitute for the divine is effected. The gods that are named, identified, and characterized give way to an unnamable and formless divine register (neither anthropomorphic nor zoomorphic, amorphous). Even before Plato, some Greeks believed that the mythological gods were fictions and that there was a single and unknowable god.

The sacred as some place in the world—on mountains, in springs, and the like—slowly gets eclipsed at the same time as its connection to human beings—through sacrifice, above all human sacrifice—also fades. Two invalidations or sublimations—admittedly different—of human sacrifice take place on the two sides of our origin: the sacrifice of Isaac and that of Iphigenia. Later, two lives will offer themselves to be immolated according to two modes of assumption or purification of sacrificial violence: Socrates and Jesus.

In the same way, according to a kind of disjointed symmetry, two unique gods absorb the divine into an incalculable remove, into what will later be called a transcendence. In truth, their uniqueness has less to do with their number than with what is their essential exclusivity. The other gods are not gods: they are not worthy.

The divine is excluded from the world, from its figures, its forces, its affects. Or rather this is how a world emerges as a "this world," distinct from a "beyond." A kind of exclusion or expulsion from inside the world is produced in which gods, humans, living beings, and inert matter had previously lived a common life.

But the phenomenon takes on two very different appearances. On the one side, it has to do with discerning the true form of things. This is a matter of directing and adjusting the gaze. True forms are called *ideas*, that is, aspects or forms offered to the eye. On the other, things are entirely different: this is a call to be heard. It asks to be listened to, which is *shema* ("listen") in Hebrew, and of course it speaks to someone, whom it calls *Israel*.

Because the call comes from elsewhere and what it wants to make heard is new, it will be spoken of later as "revelation," but we must understand that what is revealed here is above all the revealing itself: the voice that calls, declares itself, and declares what its call demands.[9]

We would need to analyse at length how both sides ended up being joined together when the god of Israel was reinterpreted as *logos*—that is, in Christianity. But, for now, what matters is the very singular conjunction *and* disjunction of the two sides of a phenomenon that, over the course of a few centuries, initiates a complete transformation of the Mediterranean world from which the history of the world—world, in both senses of "global" and "worldly"—will open up. A phenomenon occurs, has two completely heterogeneous sides, and concludes with a synthesis, as it were: this is how the history of the West still had to begin.

What is common to the Greek side and to the Jewish side is the deposing of the gods and of the sacred. There is also an anthropological inflection here that is profoundly new: rather than being inserted into an order of sacred powers, the human is found to have a capacity for autonomy in front of and with his peers (the "free people") on the one hand and, on the other, to be responsible for a call come from altogether elsewhere [*un Tout-ailleurs*].

On both sides, a sort of an emancipation takes place. Knowledge is found to be present even in Plato's slave (who therefore is emancipated in this respect), while the call directed at Israel is also the one that led it out of slavery. One might be tempted to say that there is a common revelation here: that of the human, the human freed from modes of belonging that are hierarchical, according to all the values of that word (the sacred, its power, the social order founded upon it, belonging and dependence before any kind of independence, even without any independence at all). Of course, reality cannot be reduced to this schema, especially not over the long course of centuries during which this transformation occurred. But it did happen and, far from dealing with the appearance of a new religion in Christianity, we are actually witnessing the birth of a new human.

Finally, the revelation becomes even less religious when we consider how it comes to be distinguished from the mythological regime: the Bible is not a repository of myths, even if it resembles one in some respects (especially the Book of Genesis). It is the account of the Covenant that begins from what preceded it and already contains YHWH's first address to the human being. (Lacoue-Labarthe pointed out the non-mythological character of Judaism several times. This was a theme of central importance to him, one that he shared especially with Blanchot).

In that respect, how can we fail to notice that the *logos* itself also implies the denigration of myths? The two movements are of course distinct in many respects, but the myth Plato designates as mendacious and unserious possesses the same characteristics as the "idol" that is so strongly condemned in Judaism.

7

Incompatibility

At the same time, however, the two sides of this new human being are not compatible. One is the free person of the city-state, the other is the person who is called upon. One side presents itself as autonomous, the other as heteronomous. One is destined to extend its model (universal, by definition), the other is destined to protect itself by responding to the call. This incompatibility takes hold not only between peoples; we have reason to believe that it actually structures the new human.

It is not by chance that Paul proclaims the elimination of differences between slave and freeborn, man and woman, Jew and Greek: the Christian vow reinforces only what it seeks to overcome. Beyond doubt, the incompatibility is important, not only in terms of the gap between the two claims of heteronomy and autonomy but also in terms of the much more complex deep reality that makes it such that the two sides call out to each other—and, for that to happen, also tend to push up against each other. Autonomy cannot be complete if the autonomous subject must ultimately refer to an outside of her own sphere, to a "good" that is "beyond what is given," or to a truth whose ultimate authority is as blinding as the glare of the sun or death. For its part, heteronomy is meaningful only in terms of the call through which the subject becomes herself, even if this means responding, as Abraham did, to that which she can neither understand nor accept. She is constituted in and through her trusting abandonment.

The entire western history of thought and spirituality will have been worked by the interminable, undecidable complexity of this division and contradiction within the new human. Christianity represented an extraordinary effort to take on and overcome the opposition: it put the god in the human and destined the human for the divine life. This is how the Roman world, ensnared in itself, disoriented by its own expansion and by its own power, thought to find a way out of what, at the same time, carried it outside itself.

At the moment when Judaism metamorphosed into Christianity—this moment that lasted several centuries—it was no doubt unavoidable that a break in continuity should occur. The call was in the vocative: Abraham! Israel! Without having to wait for Christianity, this naming had already angered other peoples with its air of exclusivity. Israel was taunted (for example, by having a cult of the donkey attributed to it that was later reintroduced against Christians). It would take a long time before the motif of chosenness would come to be thought of, in Christianity but also within Judaism itself, as that of a choice addressed to all by way of one alone. But even this may not be enough to suspend the opposition between one and all: if the god of the one must be the god of all, this can happen only if he is the god of each one (people or individual).

In this different way, an incompatibility emerged that did not fall under the ordinary exclusion of peoples among themselves. This one operates in a centrifugal mode: each one pushed the other, while Israel tended more to cut itself off from *goyim*—a term whose translation by *ethnai* in Greek and then by *gentiles* in Latin shows that it was understood in the sense of a belonging that is both a lineage and an institution. But the Hebrew people has its lineage and its institution within itself, through its call, in a manner that cannot be compared to any other. This is why, from the very outset, it appeared as a strangeness that had far less to do with such and such a "god" than with the entire relation of the human to the divine.[10]

This would therefore mean that the heteronomy of the Hebrew people bestows upon it a singular autonomy: an independence from any belonging or membership other than that of its response, that is, of its faithfulness. One could say that Revelation—as well as the revelation of a god—is the revelation to themselves of the ones who respond to the call. In this revelation, they are excluded from belonging in general: they belong to that which withdraws from belonging. This is also what can be heard in the phrase of a philosopher who speaks of "belonging without belonging" to his native Judeity: Derrida.

In a way, incompatibility turns out to be internal to such a subject. It is even tempting to suggest that this is exactly whence the so-called subject has come, since Hegel: the non-identity of the self with what does not rest in itself ("substance") but is supported by the other (whatever that might be). We will not be surprised to hear Freud declare that his own Jewishness remains as enigmatic as it is undeniable.

Something like an internal exclusion, an exclusion included within the structure, is thus developed. And if this development answers to the profound mutation of the relations of belonging from which the Greek city-state also emerged, the internal exclusion remains, by contrast, fundamentally foreign to the arrangement according to *logos*, because the latter returns to itself even when it designates a beyond that it names "god" or "good." Return to self or exposure to the outside: the incompatibility lies right there, at the heart of what brings together the two sides of the mutation that occurred the first centuries of our era.

8

Judeo-Christianity

Although this incompatibility was already producing some reactionary effects in the Greco-Roman world—whose axiom still involves a claim of compatibility, even in terms of advances made into the immeasurable, be it mathematical or territorial—the fact remains that what we might call a constitutive or structural hostility to Judaism first appears with Christianity. But it is also in Christianity that the catalyst of a new civilization is found.

We can identify two initial reasons for anti-Judaism. If I can put it this way, both are impassioned.

The first passion is precisely that of compatibility. As has been said, Christianity is the product

of a powerful energy, devoted (as it were) to ena-
bling a form of existence that lacks affiliations
with the gods, the sacred, and forces.[11] Harmony
is required in all things; and this motif, adopted
from the Greek world, now takes on an affective
force: Christian love, this love that the god himself is, represents the desperate will to resist what
is experienced as a dislocation of the world.

No doubt the world emerging from the
upheavals of the twelfth century BCE (the era that
saw the collapse of empires in the Middle East)
was found to be disused [*désaffecté*] in two senses
of the word: without use and without passion.
Plato's *erōs* devotes its passion to the beautiful—
to harmony, to compatibility; *philia* in the
city-state, or a city-state turned toward *sophia*,
undoubtedly lacks force (just as our notion of
"brotherhood" always lacks it, as well as our soli-
darities, or our modes of "living together").

The world of great logical skill and technical
prowess was without passion. Christian love was
inexhaustible. "Charity" refers to the recognition
of the priceless value of those we cherish. This
love itself comes from Judaism. It is related to the
call, as one aspect of it: the gods never demanded
love, nor offered it; at the most, they sometimes

united with mortals. Love changes its nature, at least in part, because it addresses itself to the other as other and blends into what is called "faith"—fidelity to the otherness of the other. Greek love, one might say, profoundly changes the lover, but does not address itself to the inestimable and unfathomable other in the beloved.

When love becomes God himself, it tends to identify the other and therefore to reduce its otherness. Christianity risks assimilating the other to the same: *interior intimo meo et superior summo meo* ["more inward than my innermost and higher than my uppermost"], the very famous expression of Augustine, contains the feat—and the promise—of a passage from the one into the other, of an infinite compatibility of the infinitely incompatible.

Christianity refuses the distance in Judaism from which the call comes. It refuses that distance with passion, since what essentially matters to it is an elimination of all distances, an immediacy (the result of a mediation) according to which the final reconciliation of an eternal life may be envisaged. Through this initial reasoning, Judaism becomes the object of disaffection.

The second passion is more devastating. As a

transformed Judaism, having passed through a Greek conception but, for all that, not having lost the distinctive features of its origin, Christianity lacks the means to affirm itself. Regardless of its ingenuity, it knows that it is dependent upon Judaism—and in a very direct way, since it is, to begin with and for a long time, only a form or a branch of Judaism. It is also dependent on philosophers and in classical antiquity is sometimes referred to as a "philosophy." But philosophy is an assimilable food. Things are different with faith. Faith is, above all, trust without guarantees. The development of Christian dogmas—incarnation, resurrection, redemption, trinity—simultaneously draws upon the resources of speculation and those of mystery. If the Christian faith admits to showing signs of its own origin from time to time, it becomes even more crucial for it to assert its autonomy.

In fact the tension between autonomy and heteronomy gets replayed at this level as well. As Greek and Roman, Christianity seeks to be self-grounding. So, where its Jewish origins are concerned, Christianity must break from its lineage; and in order to do that it must declare that the Jews did not recognize the true Messiah. In that context, at the very least, Jews are thought to be blinkered; at the most, they are considered dangerous, and also guilty of their own blindness.

Thus hostility toward Judaism—which immediately means "toward the Jews," since the people is intrinsically bound up in its Covenant: *They are the people of their god, whereas up until that time, the gods were gods of their peoples*—this kind of hostility constitutes a dimension of Christianity. And, since it is aimed at a people who have already been singled out among the "Gentiles," it will seek to overdetermine this people—inseparable from its faith—with ethnic and moral characteristics, long before races are invented.

For centuries, then, in the best-case scenario, the Jews will be thought of as the poor wretches who have been led away from the true God; and, in the worst-case scenario, they will be seen as schemers determined to fight against him. At best, Christians will wish for them to convert— the very best minds desired this over and over again; and, at worst, they will wish for their disappearance. To go that far, all that needs to be done is to invent an Aryan ideology and replace all notions of transcendence (thus Christian transcendence as well as that of metaphysics)

49

with the immanence of a techno-mythological domination. The uniqueness of the extermination of the Jews of Europe does not lie primarily in the violence deployed—the extent of violence in the twentieth century, and now in the twenty-first, is a consequence of what is called the "Anthropocene": a world where human beings find themselves alone, facing themselves in the heavens [*cieux*] and at the bottom of the oceans, on ice floes or in lithium mines. Its uniqueness has to do with what an entire history and an entire culture claim to be refounding by destroying themselves.

As if that history and that culture understood that the intimate contradiction that founds and animates them has reached a point where it has to confess: the new human has not come, but the time of the "last man" (Nietzsche) has arrived. This contradiction must finally be done away with (and therefore, it must be repeated, Christianity must also be done away with), along with basically anything that is not force and domination unleashed with no regard whatsoever for any kind of autonomy or heteronomy, let alone for their secret conflict.[12]

9

Self-loathing

This isolation of humans, alone with themselves—
the loneliness of beings who know neither what
they are nor what they do, nor the fate of the
universe they inhabit—is the most remarkable
product of the civilization that began under the
three-fold auspices of the Greeks, the Jewish,
and the Romans. Even the production of these
entities or figures—Greeks, Jewish, Romans—is
itself already the result of a transformation that
is just as difficult to explain as all the others that
have punctuated the long duration of the world.
The emancipation and then the isolation of "the
human" are without reason.

Nor is it really possible to explain the emergence of Europe, and then of the West, which

has led to a worldwide disorientation within the span of a few centuries and whose spirit—if not destiny—appears to be shaped by the inhuman loneliness of humans.

At least, though, it is not impossible to discern this characteristic feature: Europe—or the West, for here they are interchangeable—was engendered by a conjunction that was also a contradiction, namely the invention of a human type: the subject of an autonomy proper to it and, simultaneously, of a heteronomy no less its own (unless it would be more accurate to say: the subject of both its propriety and its impropriety). This type is the one we ended up naming "the subject," whether we mean that in a legal, psychological, or metaphysical sense.

The double constitution implies that one side repels the other. Whether this is refusal or denial, the subject or the European does not want to know anything about one of the sides, or even about the duality itself. This internal conflict does not prevent the subject from being enterprising and productive. On the contrary, internal conflict is the very spring of the powerful initiative and productivity that characterizes the subject. Autonomy demands that this subject become master and possessor of nature, while heteronomy demands that the same subject channel all initiative toward whatever is governed by an ideal (an accomplishment, a superhuman pleroma). Each demand constantly invalidates the other.

The incompatibility of the two sides—combined with the more visible and effective power of autonomy—has given rise to the perhaps unique phenomenon of the internal exclusion of a representative of the second side: the Jew. A unique representative—and therefore immediately set apart, because it is on the side of uniqueness that the Jew has already been identified, even invented.

Just as they withdraw from "nations," Jews are also cut off from them. This exclusion does not generate another nation. One could say that it is a question of a nation without nationalism, that is, a nation not closed off in its own strength and magnitude but from the outset intended for a "supranational responsibility" (I borrow these words and this thinking from Martin Buber's 1921 speech entitled "Nationalism").[13] In any case, this constitutes an internal exclusion. The entire history of European Jews, of the various forms of their social relegation and moral denigration, stems from that initial transformation. In forming the subject, or in forming itself as a subject, Europe divided that subject into a light and a dark part, distributed between conquest of the world and growing confusion in the face of this very conquest.

As we know, Rousseau is the central figure in the reorientation of reason, of reason casting doubt upon itself. It is not by chance that he is also one of the few admirers of the longevity and steadfastness of the Jewish people over the course of so many ages and amid so many possible causes of disintegration. After him, through the complex and otherwise perverse process that organizes this entire history, the Jews start being designated as the agents of European degeneration.

Antisemitism is "historial" and "spiritual" because it is inextricably tied to a history that has come to lose its own direction or purpose, precipitating the autonomy that fueled its energy in doubt and panic. The Jew will have served as the scapegoat for everything that, for a very long time, this history experienced or at least adumbrated as an impasse. The Jew will have been to blame for everything that modern Europe or the West hates about itself and continues to brood over:

for its hatred of money, hatred of power, hatred of democracy, hatred of technology—all of which are of course coupled with a corresponding and yet necessarily miserable love. Christian churches have very often exemplified this ambivalence.

In the history of Mediterranean Europe, Islam might serve as counterproof: inasmuch as it, too, is tied to western history, it is distinguished from it by the distance it maintained from the project of European rationality, which began quite early on (even if, much later, it joined that project in its own way). But Islam was not familiar with anti-semitism, at least not in the Christian European way. Antisemitism has not been a permanent feature of Islam or an obsession throughout its history. Only the creation of the State of Israel under the auspices of Europe has unleashed a sys-tematic hostility. But Islam did not have to assert itself against its own origin. It comported itself as an independent successor would, and not as a son or a younger brother in the grips of jealousy.

Nevertheless, the creation of Islam did take place in close proximity to Judaism and Christianity—the entirety of the Qur'an dem-onstrates this—and therefore it, too, received something of the Christian hostility to Judaism.

This hostility can be discerned in that same text. The accusations against Israel found there are clearly echoes of Christian accusations.

In Europe today, the antisemitism (carelessly mixed with anti-Zionism) of fundamentalist (and reactionary) Christians fuels the hostility of Muslims toward Jews.

10

Mutation

In cases of paranoia, it often happens that a threat emerging from the self is transformed into a threat coming from another—present, visible, and audible—who desperately wants what I have, my possessions, my person, or my image. The subject of Europe acted in just such a paranoid way regarding Israel, which was one of its fathers, or its older brother. Its own self excludes within itself that aspect of itself that is hidden away in the unprecedented conception—said of the one God—of a heteronomy that is chosen, resolute, and responsible. Putting an end to this exclusion cannot be done without a substantial change to what has entered history under the name of Europe and then of the West—which in turn becomes the name of an exclusion from self that is today broader still. From every direction, then, the subject of civilization—or of progress, technology, democracy, art, and so on—denounces itself precisely to the same extent as it asserts itself through the expansion of its power and control.

It denounces itself, specifically—that is, in an essential way—*as a subject*: all the criticisms or deconstructions, all the divisions or catastrophes of the "subject" that take place in modern thought attest to a painful relationship of auto-immunity of this subject with itself.

Everyday humanity calls itself senseless; and it does so either because it must endure too many evils, injustices, or humiliations or because it is drunk on an excessiveness that goes beyond all common measure and to which, for better or worse, its own powers have exposed it.

One might think that self-destruction of this ambit and intensity goes so far beyond antisemitism that it runs the risk of minimizing it or of causing it to be forgotten. On the contrary, it is only by discerning the historial and spiritual stakes of a hatred that accompanies the entire course of our history that we may be able to subject this course to a transformation as profound as that from which antisemitism arose.

Antisemitism is inseparable from the self-hatred of the subject because this phantasmatic subject, "the Jew," *represents very precisely the inverted figure of the Subject*: "a people sure of itself and domineering," said de Gaulle in an unintentional self-portrait, a genius in business and calculation on a global scale, ambitious and greedy. Is this not the accursed self-image that the West projects onto its scapegoat, in an endless ritual of conjuration by exclusion?

II

Drives

In the final analysis (if it is possible to go that far . . .), what is such a complex configuration about—or one so *twisted*, to say it with all the perspicuity of this familiar (banal, vulgar) word? What is such a contortion, convulsion, hideous grimace about, stamped as it is from the beginning on the face of a civilization that was the first (and perhaps the last) to become global or, alternatively, cosmic? To what should we relate such a singularly pernicious and self-destructive characteristic of what will have been the first (and perhaps the last) invention of the "universal"? And how could we give an account, no matter how limited, of what will have been the first exercise in mass murder, one organized, planned, and calculated with such cold and delusional fury?

It is not enough to invoke the transition to the modern dimensions of technology, domination, and racism, as I have just done here. This change of scale, however, is certainly not irrelevant: whatever separates the *Adversus Iudaeos* homilies of the first centuries, the fifteenth-century expulsion of the Jews from Spain, and the pogroms of the nineteenth century from the Nazi "Final Solution," taken as a whole, constitutes a series of crossings or excesses from one era to the next and the constant pursuit of the same motif: that of a curse or a burden justified by God, by history, by the need to rid the world of an abominable stain linked to the constitution and malignant obstinacy of a people whose permanence alone already arouses suspicion.

What is noticeable about this combination of shifts and progressions is that each of the steps is accompanied by a historic upheaval: the fall of Rome, the crusades, the birth of capitalism and of the New World, the industrial and scientific age, the time of the masses and of "disenchantment." Each of these tremors takes place through a play of forces that shake up an established order turned disorder and social discontent. Each time, it is a world that cracks and collapses. Each time, it is a kind of drive or impulse that upsets the state of things, customs, and minds.

The first of these upheavals is the one—both Greek and Jewish, inextricably—that brought about the end of a world governed by the powers of order, hierarchy, organization, and discipline. The western upheaval involves all these ensembles, whose ordering (relative, to be sure) ensured a mastery, a system of channels, and a regulated expression of the forces of rupture, antagonism, and destruction exercised at the deepest level of life itself and, still more, of the existence of living speaking beings. This is not the place to dwell on it: the experience of today's world—and the banalized exception of antisemitism within it—is formed essentially through bitter awareness of this violence that lives within us.

Capitalism, the conquest of the world, colonization, the harnessing of energies, the conquest of space, and the exploitation of the masses are successive stages of this violence—accompanied as it was by the magnificent appearance of so many works of knowledge and art—in which the Jews will certainly have played no small part.

Since its beginning, our civilization has been concerned to suppress the appetites, to control the passions, to repress the drives. Finally, Freud will wonder whether this repression itself might not have been excessive, since he sees it as resulting in extremes of violence where humanity becomes a threat to itself.

Greek *logos*—order and knowledge—and Jewish faith—trust and observance—emerge together, opposed yet convergent, separate yet close by, as a double movement destined to replace the ancient powers of ordering. It is a double effort for an autonomy freed from subjugation; but this autonomy must discover its own law. On the one hand, it seeks that autonomy in itself; on the other, it discovers it in a covenant with another.

Christianity attempts a synthesis, which, however, opens up a violent disruption. It is not a coincidence that the drives of renunciation, asceticism, and submission are intensified through that synthesis, as well as other drives to control and denigrate the passions. Nor is it a coincidence that the "death of God" corresponds to a reinvestment in what was called *instinct* before it was named *drive*: from Sade and Kant to Hitler and Freud, a very deep disorder continues in its double tack, panic-stricken or worried, escalating or wanting to subside.

Antisemitism speaks the dark truth of a world conceived in a conjunction that is originally disjunctive. That world must henceforth make another one possible—or else it will destroy itself.

Antisemitic God

When asked whether there was any concrete proof of God's existence, Voltaire replied: "Yes, the Jews." Voltaire considered the Jews to be the "most detestable nation to have ever sullied the earth."[14] So, it was the persistence of defilement that would ultimately prove the existence of God. As we know, Voltaire's god is only a watchmaker: his existence is proven by permanence—even if that be the permanence of what is most hideous.

This is an object lesson in how poorly European reason resolves the contradictions that structure it.

When dialectics seeks to overcome the contradictions, it makes them into a terrible metaphysical destiny: for Hegel, the meaning of the Jewish people is to be found in the testimony they provide that spirit only finds itself through the pain of its own division. The Jews demonstrate the misery endured by the world spirit. (Hegel does not yet envisage their disappearance: for him, as for Augustine and Pascal before him, they are necessary witnesses.)

When one experiences the contradiction as a natural condition of our culture (and of our psyche), one can, along with the Jewish Freud, make a witty remark and say that God, in a moment of antisemitism, produced a son of the finest Jewish extraction.

As if Freud sensed in God a self-loathing? But this is just a joke!

Yet is it not precisely Freud who says that a funny remark is often the way to get an unpleasant truth across?

God: either the perfect autonomy, the fundamental *logos*, the power of life and death, the overwhelming illusion, domination, the god of metaphysics, or else the perfect heteronomy, the Creator, Father, and Judge before whom one bows and beats one's breast, the God of religion, the one and the other excluding another, their other, an unnamable, an ineffable, a breath, an invisible face, an absence that leaves us wandering aimlessly away from absent sense—delivers us to our simple, and unheard-of, humanity.

To be done with it. . .

Artaud wanted *to do away with the judgment of God*: to be done with that, though, we must do away with antisemitism—we must do away with the deadly face to face, as well as with the murderous alliance, within God, of the two principles of autonomy and heteronomy and the gangrene of their confrontation.

We must do away with principles, with the principle of trusting in principles (in "origins," "natures," "subjects") because in principle it excludes, expels, and exterminates. It alone makes possible not only antisemitism, but every kind of racism. Our civilization became racist only because it carried the seed of it to begin with. But it is itself in the process of excluding itself from the very idea of "civilization," and every expectation (if not every hope) is possible.

Additional notes

1

An originary division means that an origin is divided, just as much as it means that a division is originary. Both meanings must be explored and examined together.

A divided origin is still *one* origin. The division happens to it, which is to say that it happened to *it*, that the division comes after. This is how many origins represent a division, complication, contradiction, or decline that happens later. Such is the case with the most famous of origins in our culture: original sin that befalls creation. It is a modification of creation, and at the same time it constitutes a new origin.

The fall of Phaeton, as Plato's Critias reports

it from Solon in the *Timaeus*, constitutes such a division of the cosmic origin, to which corresponds, in the human register, the fall of the bad horse in Plato's *Phaedrus*. The two stories, the nature of each, and their characters are all very different. (One could even say that the opposition between autonomy and heteronomy is already implicit in them.) The fact remains that a type of accident seems to affect the origins of the West.

But is the origin itself not specifically western, especially if one understands Egypt as the origin of this regime of origins (particularly according to Memphite cosmogony)? In other cultures it is most often a case of operations that claim to order a primitive chaos, itself given from the beginning of time. This given chaos is not entirely absent from Genesis—it is the *tohu wa-bohu*, which is without form and void—but it is not reshaped to be put into order: the creator suddenly makes the world appear, independently of it. The difference is not between chaos and order, but between a sterile emptiness and an invigorating breath.

If this is so, the origin specific to the West divides itself into two and obliges us to consider the hypothesis of an originary division: on the one hand, creation out of nothing; on the other, the only true origin that is the logos (it pre-exists or presides over the world; these two notions are equivalent). In other words, a heteronomy and an autonomy. On both sides there is a fall, but the first one stems from betraying the creator, while the second involves an imbalance that can be rectified by the very subject affected by this imbalance.

2

The previous note prompts us to ask whether it is even appropriate to speak of an originary structure of the West: perhaps we should rather think of the West (or, if we prefer, of "western-ness") as the condition for the emergence of the form and structure of the origin. Westernness would be what happens to a world for which there could only ever be a given, never a pure origin: given gods or given elements—available presences without destination. By contrast, origin implies direction, sending, destination. The West is destined or destinal. Tragedy revolves around this: impenetrable destinies, a destinal impenetrability. The *logos* or the covenant: two irreconcilable attempts to overcome tragedy, one through autonomy, the other through a kind of hetero-autonomy.

3

A lexical point might be of interest here. Since Kant, we have become accustomed to opposing autonomy to heteronomy. From a Greek point of view, this opposition is poorly formed: the opposite of *autos* ("same") is *allos* ("other"), which designates the otherness of another in a set or series (of things, of persons, of terms, etc.); the opposite of *heteros* ("other") is *homos* ("same"), which designates an identity of nature, of genus, or of content. In opposing *autos* to *heteros*, intentionally or not, we are killing two birds with one stone: the law of heteronomy is not just given by another human, it comes from *an other than human*. To spin it in these terms, it is not democratic but hierarchical. But doing this disregards the idea that the otherness of the "god" in question, like that of the Kantian "moral law" for that matter, is less that of an other-than-human and much more that of the absolute "other," which proclaims itself to the human in the human: in which case it would be an instance of *allos* more than one of *heteros*.

It is no coincidence that the most general form of the questions inherent in democracy (which in fact forms part of the definition of the West) concerns the possibility or impossibility of combining equality and authority. We have difficulty conceiving of the idea, much less receiving it, that authority belongs to our own alterity to ourselves.

4

Judaism's own history is itself woven out of a contradiction between autonomy and heteronomy. Heteronomous by virtue of its covenant with the God who gives his law to his people, it is also autonomous by virtue of its distinction from other peoples and by virtue of the equality among all the sons of Israel (which, moreover, implies an equality between all the sons of man and woman, whether or not they are part of the Covenant). But the autonomy of Israel—as soon as it comes to be less about the people and more about the kingdom—is forever attracted to forgetting the Covenant. The prophet before the king, or the people turning to idolatry represents a fundamental confrontation from which internal divisions emerge at the time of the first diasporas, one of which will become Christianity;

and there the same confrontation is indefinitely revived. Moreover, this confrontation is coupled with the rejection of its origin in the name of a higher autonomy, which in itself will keep being divided in many ways . . . even to the point of opposing God to God.

5

The very difficult and complex question of the present State of Israel bears the most visible signs of a recurrence of the same confrontation, reconfigured after the persecution and extermination of Christian, Roman, and imperial origins (to reach the Third Reich, one could relate this to what has already been said about empire in the Introduction) and after the already long history of prophetism, which was assumed to encompass and relativize its predecessors—Islam presenting the Prophet in the most literal sense of the word: the one through whom God speaks.

Palestinian autonomy is, rightfully, indisputable for Jewish faith or thought, while the need to protect a people that the madness of exclusion has made into a destinal victim risks getting lost in the forgetting of the covenant that was mentioned earlier.

The current outburst of Muslim antisemitism is not surprising, especially considering the entire history of the three-fold monotheism of the West, that is, the multiple avatars of the profound internal contradiction of history, or of the subject called "Europe," then "the West," and then, finally, "the World" ...

6

In an unexpected, even bewildering, and yet intelligible way, antisemitism—the self-hatred of the West—spreads its poison to this "globe," which finally knows nothing about autonomy or heteronomy any more. This is also why we should come back—much more than I was able to do here—to the contemporaneity of Auschwitz and Hiroshima, as well as to the terrible accumulation of total wars, genocides, and ideological and cultural miseries that are our burden today.

Notes

1 Only in Japan can one find a similar desire, no doubt also tied to obsessions with refoundation.

2 The great poet Louis Zukofsky, always so attentive and so demanding in his thinking (along with others) about Judaism, cites this letter in Section 8 of his epic poem *"A"*: see Louis Zukofsky, *"A."* Los Angeles: University of California Press, 1978: 71.

3 Claudio Magris, *Blameless*, trans. Anne Milano Appell. New Haven, CT: Yale University Press, 2017: 221.

4 Or the horror of other (earlier, simultaneous, or subsequent) genocides, the nature of which and possible links to the genocide of the Jews I am not able to consider here.

5 [TN: Lacoue-Labarthe, *Heidegger, Art, and Politics: The Fiction of the Political*, trans. Chris Turner. London: Basil Blackwell, 1990: 48.]

6 I would say "transcendental," if this term were not as poorly understood as it is today.

7 The relation that this intuition has to his entire work, and even to his life, deserves a separate analysis, to be carried out elsewhere, of course.

8 [TN: *Jud Süss* (*Süss the Jew*), a Nazi German propaganda film that purported to portray the eighteenth-century German Jewish lawyer Joseph Süss Oppenheimer.]

9 It would be necessary to dwell on the character of the roughly contemporaneous phenomena in Asia represented by the names of Siddhartha Gautama on the one hand and Lao Tzu on the other. It is inevitable that we should find similarities, despite important differences. I should also touch on Zoroastrianism, which we know had certain relations of filiation with Christianity through Manichaeism. What is certain is that all these phenomena during the first millennium BCE indicate a time of anthropological transformation for a not insignificant part of humanity. Similarly, one should dwell on historical or protohistoric hypotheses about the formation of the Hebrew people from slave populations fleeing from collapsing empires. All this exceeds the limits of a brief essay.

10 To limit myself to two major contemporary philosophical references, both Adorno and Steiner clearly understood that "monotheism" was at first a barely tolerable intrusion in the Mediterranean world. One

could say that it was the intrusion within itself of the exclusion of self.

11 I shall not dwell on the fact that, in every respect, Christianity also reconstitutes a whole set of properly religious guarantees, intercessions, and divine or hagiological protections. In this respect, it will divide itself from itself at the time of the Reformation, which was another way of dividing the subject again, or even of reinventing it by exacerbating its internal division. In the context of the Reformation, Judaism will be understood not so much as an exposure to the call, but rather in terms of how ignorant it is of the true message; and this ignorance will henceforth be connected to a character that is abominable, cynical, pleasure-seeking, and diabolical and whose phantasmatic creation says a great deal about the devils that swarm about within the good Christian.

12 I cannot pause here over the contrasting parallel that would have to be developed, as regards antisemitism, with that other "totalitarian" undertaking (in this case the "total" character consists mainly in allowing no kind of disparity, contradiction, or incompatibility).

13 It is starting from here that it would be necessary to take up the complex and delicate questions that arise around the State of Israel, the genesis of which— need we be reminded?—included some measure of antisemitism.

14 [TN: Voltaire, *Dictionnaire philosophique* [1764], in
   Louis Moland, ed., *Voltaire: Oeuvres complètes* (52
   vols.). Paris, 1877–85: vol. 20, 517–18.]